Awakening
THE DEEP SLEEP

VICTORIA BOYSON

Awakening

THE DEEP SLEEP

AWAKENING: THE DEEP SLEEP
Copyright © 2014
All Rights Reserved.
Published by Kingdom House Press
ISBN 978-0-990608-00-4

Victoria Boyson Ministries
www.victoriaboyson.com
victoria@boyson.org

CONTENTS

CONTENTS

FOR DANIEL

And do this, understanding the present time: The hour has already come for you to wake up from your slumber, because our salvation is nearer now than when we first believed. The night is nearly over; the day is almost here. So let us put aside the deeds of darkness and put on the armor of light.

—Romans 13:11-12 NIV

Introduction

Dear Friends,

THE LORD IS as creative in communicating His truths to us as He is in designing His creation. I believe the visions and dreams He gives us are a lot like the parables He gave in the Bible, in which He teaches us His truths through stories. Many people, including myself, learn His truth best from parables and visions that help clarify the Word.

This book is a series of visions the Lord has given me over several years. As He would call me to a visionary encounter with Him, it felt very much like being called to a visionary journey. I've tried to make it as descriptive as I saw it, so you would feel as though you were right there with Beloved, our heroine.

I wanted to be faithful to the words He gave and the imagery He showed me so I could, without reservation, assure you it was from Him *to you*.

Over thirty years ago, my mother went to her true home in heaven's realm. Since that time, my awareness of that realm has been more than awakened, and sometimes I feel more a part of it than of earth.

One of my favorite Scriptures is Colossians 3:1-3, "If then you have been raised with Christ, seek the things that are above [in heaven], where Christ is, seated at the right hand of God. Set your minds on things that are above, not on things that are on earth. For you have died, and your life is hidden with Christ in God" (ESV, emphasis mine).

In this life, I've found true reality only as I've experienced this life "hidden with Christ," living not for a temporal purpose but for the eternal goals of God's heavenly kingdom. His kingdom is as real as the world we live in and as we seek to know Him better, we will learn of His kingdom, becoming stewards of the kingdom of heaven on earth.

For years, at times I've felt my mother's strength with me, but in recent days I've felt much more than that. When I think of her now, it is not a memory or recollection of what she was like in her life on earth, but it is as I have seen her only in my dreams – a woman filled with great power and with the purpose of the kingdom she belongs to.

In these moments with her it's as though she, and with her the entire heavenly kingdom, is urging me to remain **wide awake** – faithful to my focused earthly-purpose and keeping watchful for the tricks that can dull the senses in this world.

This is something new and different than I have ever felt before. I feel shaken by the true reality of her realm. It's as though the Lord has allowed her just one moment to speak to me of something of such eternal importance, and her urgency is alarming.

Dear saints, you truly are the bride of Christ and the celebration of heaven. The world has yet to see your true inner beauty and to feel the waves of piercing glory that will burst forth from your love for Jesus.

The glory of God is made tangible to the world by the light of His love emanating through you. That love WILL spread to the farthest corners of the earth, canvassing it in His beauty.

The Lord says to you, "Awaken, my love, it is time to awaken."

—Victoria

I

The Deep Sleep

Time is running out. Wake up, for our salvation is nearer now than when we first believed.
—Romans 13:11 NLT

IT WAS DUSK when Beloved awoke and, standing
in the middle of a vast sea of wildflowers, she saw pur-
ple and pink blossoms as far as her eyes could reach.
Her mind was filled with confusion, making her unsure
of where she was or why she was there.

Before her lay rolling fields of beautiful flowers, yet
there was an ominous weightiness in the atmosphere
that disturbed her. The remains of slumber tried its best
to cloud her vision and pull her back to sleep, to over-
whelm her with its lethargy. Beloved struggled to shrug

off the drag of numbness she felt in her mind as she fought to comprehend the truth of her situation.

As the reality of her condition set in, she realized she had been asleep. She didn't remember having fallen asleep but did recall a faint dream she'd had that had awoken her. It had been about a world in desperate need for her help – she knew she was needed, but by whom and for what purpose?

Beloved noticed the flowers she stood in and was immediately made quite aware of the sinister scene all around her. Studying more closely, she discovered people lying fast asleep in the flowers. She stared in amazement at thousands of men and women, even some children, sleeping amongst the captivating field of blossoms.

The landscape was so stunningly beautiful it took her breath away. Yet in it lay a whole world of people sleeping as though they'd been caught in the middle of their lives.

Her shock compelled her to wonderment. As if being drawn into their lives, Beloved felt the urge to discover who or what had caused this plague of slumber.

She sensed that many of those asleep had, at one time in their lives, clarity of destiny, yet had lost their way. Stopping too long, they were caught by the lull and beauty of the flowers until they could no longer remember their purpose and fell captive to an unshakeable sleep.

The immensity of what seemed to her to be an unparalleled epidemic of afflicted narcosis sent her mind whirling.

"Were they held captive by the pull of the world?" she wondered as questions flooded her heart.

Beloved stood bewildered, watching and questioning. While she was preoccupied with the mystery of what she was experiencing, she suddenly realized she was being watched.

Startled, she swung around and discovered, standing quite near her, a large, beaming, angelic being full of light and wonder. Watching her, his warm eyes waited expectantly, as if wanting her to notice him.

He was radiant with an intensely brilliant yet tranquil light and something about him made her feel completely comfortable in spite of his astonishing appearance. Something in Beloved gave her the feeling she had always known him ... he seemed quite familiar.

Stunned by his magnificence, she stepped back to adjust to the alarming affect he had on her. Looking at him with large, wondering eyes, she instinctively felt he seemed to be waiting for something.

As if in response to her unspoken questions, he motioned out over the endless scene and asked, "Will you help us?"

"Us?" Beloved questioned.

He seemed surprised at her question. "Yes, us," he answered as he bent down and tenderly held the hand of one sleeping woman. "We are the angelic who serve those sleeping here."

Suddenly, Beloved's eyes were opened to the extraordinary assembly of angelic beings all around her, waiting as he had been. Now in sight were thousands of beautifully bright elysian beings towering over her, radiating confident peace in spite of their concern for those asleep.

Some of the angelic knelt down to speak to those sleeping. Lovingly, yet earnestly, they tried to awaken those held captive by the deep sleep. The great care they expressed for those sleeping stirred a compassion in Beloved for them as well – she wanted to help if she could.

Looking again to the being who had addressed her, Beloved asked, "How can *I* help *you*?"

He rose and stood again beside her and said, "We've been unable to wake them because we cannot enter their world of dreams."

As she approached each precious person, her spirit felt the impressions of what their lives were like. Beloved thought for a while, then realized she had been given grace to decipher the hearts of man, yet seeing only what the Father wanted to show her. She could see glimpses into their past, present and future, and sensed the pain they'd experienced in the world they lived in.

Sitting down in the flowers near the woman whose hand the angel had clasped, Beloved was drawn to help this very sweet and gentle woman. She brushed the woman's hair from her face and felt a wave of peace as her hand grazed her face.

Beloved was then gripped by a rapid succession of pictures that flew through her mind. The woman had been an avid follower of Jesus as a child but had fallen in love very young, and an abortion in her teens had aged her and injured her heart. She still wanted God, but grew cynical and mistrustful of Him.

Though the woman grew up and eventually married, Beloved saw that she never regained the passion for her First Love. Instead, she kept up with what she felt was *expected* of her as a Christian woman and hid her true yearnings. Subsequently, she was led astray – finding her worth not in her heavenly Father but in a temporal world of power and importance.

Beloved could feel the longing in the woman's heart for something more – something real that had eluded her in her pursuits. But she had been unable to shake the sleep of the world she believed was her reality.

As Beloved knelt by the woman, she dropped her head in her hands and cried. Turning to the awaiting angelic and shaking her head, she exclaimed, "She was so close."

"Close to what?" he asked her.

"True reality," Beloved cried.

She then turned and touched the hand of a man asleep near her on her other side. She saw a large building filled with people who admired him, yet he felt empty. He was so busy running and working continually, trying desperately to attain a satisfactory measure of peace that seemed to elude him. It appeared no level of success would ever be enough to ease the force in his life that was recklessly driving him from one project to the next.

From one need to another, this man gave himself to his work. Only occasionally in his downtime would he question himself as to what was driving him. He wondered, "Why am I still so empty?"

Beloved went from person to person, and each individual had a history of trials and successes, driven by unseen forces within them. Yet all had the internal question in their heart they had not given themselves time to dwell on: "What is this life really about?"

As they worked and lived in their perceived realities, questions drifted in and out of their thoughts only occasionally in their busyness. The questions seemed to come as the heavenly creatures tried to awaken them.

Unfortunately, as soon as they would attempt to struggle with their slumber, they were captivated again by the poisonous fragrance of the wildflowers of the world and, again, busied themselves in what they believed to be of true importance.

Overwhelmed by the seemingly beguiled condition of those caught in the deep sleep, Beloved wept. She wanted to run away but was surrounded by a crowd of the angelic who were anticipating her help.

Her face sank into her hands once again as she suddenly realized, "This is the Lord's last-days army!"

These poor, cleverly deluded people were those He was counting on to fulfill His great mandate. These noble warriors of immense importance to God were presently living in a dream reality – a distraction from their true life and purpose. Increasing her anxiety, she knew these essential warriors did not even realize they were at war.

She could see it was a clever lie for, effectively, they had forgotten who they were. They had lost sight of heaven and the reality of its realm and were, indeed, held captive in a temporal world apart from their eternal Source.

Heaven and earth are indeed one, separated only by an expanse of sky. Yet so much of the earthly world is believing its own reasonings and has rationalized its own "truth," that it belongs only to itself, existing independently from the realm of its Creator.

Unfortunately, many of this world's inhabitants found out too late they had believed a deceptive version of reality, as if living in a dream world. They lived their lives serving an illusion that this earthly life was all that mattered, without really considering its origin, and thus were driven by a tricky delusion keeping them isolated from the truth of its blessed union with heaven.

Beloved considered all she was discovering, yet it only deepened her sadness and seemed to increase the terrible difficulty she was faced with. She needed help; she could not fight this battle on her own. It was too much for her.

Sensing her burden, the angelic host drew near and comforted her with their support.

"You are not alone," they informed her.

"I'm not?"

"No, Beloved. There are other seekers just like your-self who've discovered true reality is not found in this earthly realm; they are like you and they know of you."

"Why, if they know me, do they not show them-selves?" She felt frustrated and befuddled, almost angry at hearing what he had told her.

He placed his hand gently on her shoulder and she could now see a vision of what had previously been hid-den from her. "A prophetic host!" she exclaimed with whispered excitement.

She could see in the spirit realm a relatively small but intensely powerful army of the King's seekers who were hidden in plain sight. They were concealed for their protection as well as for the significance of the bat-tle they were to fight. Many of them were even unaware of the destiny that lay before them; they had no idea of their importance.

The angel answered her thoughts, "Yes, Beloved. They are hidden. The Father has hidden them for the next great battle ... the battle to awaken His Son's pre-cious bride."

Now, seeing them through the eyes of the Spirit, she no longer felt alone. For the first time since awakening, she felt hope rise in her heart.

2

My Rock

You are my rock and my fortress. For the honor
of your name, lead me out of this danger.
—Psalm 31:3 NLT

AS THE VISION faded, she dropped to her knees.
She began to pray for the prophetic and the army of
the Lord, but especially for herself. For she knew great
difficulty lay ahead of her and she would need God's
strength.

Beloved prayed with all her soul, venting her worry
through the deep travail that poured from her heart.
She lay emotionally exhausted on the ground, interced-
ing throughout the night until at last she felt the peace
of God fill her, and she finally rested in the place she'd
fallen.

When she rose from her rest, determined compassion surged inside. It was of the utmost importance she try and find the hidden host she'd seen in her vision. Beloved didn't know exactly where to begin, but had a mysterious sense she would be guided. She was compelled to find them and, however long it may take her to get to them, she had determined to succeed.

Saying goodbye to the angelic she'd met guarding the sleeping army, she ventured on toward fields of golden wheat just outside the region of the toxic flowers. Though she felt deeply for the sleeping souls, she knew help for them would not come from her alone and was grateful to be finally leaving to find that help.

As she entered the fields, she suddenly felt such indefinable freedom, filling her with the desire to run. Away from the oppression of the sleeping army she ran with hurried strain. Wanting to run away from her worry, she wasn't sure where she was going, but was compelled to run – to put distance between herself and the upsetting burden she felt for the sleeping army.

The fields were beautifully golden and glimmered as the warm sun hit them. It lifted her spirit to be released to follow the leading of her heart, to be following the purpose she knew God had given her. Running through the tall stalks of wheat, it seemed to brush away her sorrow from the night before. She wanted to feel the joy the wheat seemed to possess, but was still caught up in the determination she felt in her assignment.

In her heart, she knew she would experience many trials in her journey, and there was a great distance to be traveled before she would encounter any sign of the host. Still, it felt good for her to begin.

As she ran through the fields, a song began to fill her heart. It was a song she remembered the angels singing over her while she rested with them, and it encouraged her. "Come to the table ... the Savior wants you to join in the feast..." (Michael Card lyrics) – over and over in her mind and spirit the special tune resonated.

Running through the fields, she was captivated by the scene surrounding her. She was completely caught off guard when it seemed something had suddenly reached up and grabbed her foot.

With a thud, she landed on the ground. Turning to see what had tripped her, what she saw puzzled her. It was a rock!

Completely surprised and bewildered, she looked all around it to see if someone had hidden behind it, but there was no one there ... there was no one anywhere.

Beloved stood alone staring at an amazingly large rock in the middle of the vast field.

"A rock? How could a rock *grab me?*" Beloved wondered.

Attempting to convince herself she had, in fact, only tripped, she sat in the middle of the large, open field and stared at the rock. In her bemusement, she pulled up some stalks of wheat and threw them toward the rock. Suddenly, she felt an outburst of laughter flood the atmosphere around her.

"Who's there?" she demanded, nearly coaxed into laughter herself, much to her own surprise.

Still and quiet, waiting to hear if someone were near her, she again heard nothing. She looked back at the rock and puzzled over it. Tilting her head to one side, she studied it curiously, noticing that she felt strangely drawn to it.

Beloved sat for a moment, then cautiously reached up to touch the rock. When she did, she felt a sear of pulsating power go through her hand. The current went up into her arm and flooded her heart. It was an amazingly powerful sensation that made her feel tremendously alive.

Surprised, she pulled her hand back and sat for some while trying to comprehend what was happening. Beloved wondered if she were just imagining what she felt, and reached up to touch the rock again. Once more, she felt the strong current of power flow into her hand, down her arm and into her heart.

All at once, she thought she recognized the source of the power she felt and whispered, "Jesus?" Yes, she was sure it was Him. In any form, she could recognize His presence. Beloved threw herself on the Rock, embracing it with all her might, and tears began to flow freely.

"Jesus," she cried. "Oh, how I needed You!"

She poured out her heart for some time until she felt Him speak to her spirit.

"Dear one," He said, "you were running through fields of grace and I had to stop you. I didn't want you to miss them."

"Miss them, Jesus? Miss what?"

"Precious Beloved, the fields of grace you've been running through are a most powerful force in My kingdom. I couldn't let you continue to run through them and miss the treasures they held."

"Treasures, Lord?"

"*My grace holds a vast wealth of treasure that cannot be rushed through. You must walk in My rest to enjoy it all – trusting Me with your burdens. As you walk through it, you enjoy Me and I you, letting grace have its complete work in you.*"

"Do you understand now?" He asked.

"Only that I need to take it easy and not rush Your work in me. Is that it?"

"AND that you *enjoy* it. It is here to be savored. *I love to watch you enjoy what I made for you.*"

"But... I just left..." she tried to interrupt Him and tell Him of the burdens in her heart.

"I know, dear one, about the burdens you carry. But know that first they were Mine and if I had not wished it, they would not be yours now. You've grown so much, Beloved, and I am extremely proud of you, but you have more to learn. You are strong enough now to carry the load I've given you, but only with My help. We'll have fun carrying it together. It's a work for us to share."

Beloved heaved a huge sigh of relief. She felt His peace flood her, enabling her heart to enjoy time spent with Him. Soaking in His peace and the release she felt, she was overwhelmed by the Lord as He captivated her heart.

3

FIELDS OF GRACE

And rejoice before the LORD your God at the
place he will choose as a dwelling for his Name —
you...   —Deuteronomy 16:11 NIV

IN HER ENCOUNTER with the Lord, Beloved
learned to yield to His wishes for her and to enjoy the
fields of grace. She walked more slowly now and took
pleasure in her journey, letting the wheat brush against
her as she moved through it. Captivated by the fresh,
earthy aromas of the field, she was warmed by the sun's
rays reflecting on the golden crop.

As she enjoyed the fields, they were having their
intended affect on Beloved, just as the Lord anticipated. Little by little, she was being restored by grace.
The worry and fear, pain and disappointment, all her

bitter feelings were being swept away with every step in God's treasured fields of grace. Much more at ease now, her spirit seemed to feel and see with a keener sensitivity than it had in the past.

Thinking she was alone, her thoughts flooded her mind. Suddenly she looked ahead in the fields and saw several laborers. Beloved was so excited to see laborers working in the fields of grace.

She knew they must have been there all the while, but she could not see them. Now, with the eyes of her spirit renewed and refreshed by the grace that sustained her, she watched them intently.

They were lucent, spirit-like people, as if they were in another dimension. As Beloved watched them openly, they did not seem to notice her at all and continued to work vigorously in the fields.

Beloved stood marveling at their work, but noticed they were dreadfully tired, and some seemed close to exhaustion. Their fatigued demeanor seemed out of place in such a peaceful place. She felt deeply burdened as she watched them work faithfully, almost methodically, gathering the harvest.

As she stared, almost mesmerized by the workers, she felt jarred by the sense of someone watching her from behind. Turning quickly to see who it was, she marveled when she saw an impressive man dressed in royal attire.

Catching her eyes in his, he greeted her as though he knew her. "Beloved," he said as he smiled with delight.

"Hello, sir," she answered, and then asked, "What are you doing here?"

"I'm following the laborers through the fields to hunt for the treasure they've left behind."

Beloved was quiet for a while. She could not understand how he would come to work in the fields dressed like a king. Then, a sudden thought sprang to her mind, "Could he be the man I've heard of?" She questioned him, "Are you the treasure hunter, sir?"

The question seemed to delight him and he laughed a cheerful, hearty laugh. As he reached down into the mud and dirt of the field, he asked, "Well, Beloved, do you think I have found treasure?"

He was holding a woman's arm and gently pulled her closer to stand near him. Beloved was truly puzzled because she had not seen the woman at all, though she'd passed right by where the woman lay.

Earnestly, he continued with his questioning and asked her again, "Is *she* treasure, Beloved?"

Beloved was simply shocked by what she saw and stood almost paralyzed. She realized she knew the woman, who was a prostitute who lived in Beloved's hometown. Beloved remembered her to be a forgotten person whose life was riddled with a heavy burden of shame, never experiencing even the simplest of joys that most people take for granted. She was someone Beloved had prayed for but out of fear had not actually talked to.

Without waiting for Beloved's answer, he asked her another question. "What about this one, Beloved. Is *he* treasure?"

She suddenly saw a man standing at his side just as the woman had – she knew him, as well. He was a man she'd met when traveling with friends. They had picked him up and given him a ride. She remembered him to be extremely careworn and burdened by life. Beloved had tried to witness to him and wanted to lead him to the Lord, but felt she had failed him.

"Yes!" she cried out in surprise.

When she had last seen him, she had been very young and was neither bold nor strong. She had missed him in the field as well, but the treasure hunter found him.

Beloved was all at once flooded with feelings of shock and relief, but the treasure hunter wasn't done yet. "Watch, Beloved," he said.

Then he drew both the man and the woman into himself, holding each of them close in his arms. Pulling them into himself, he buried their heads in his chest. He held them there for some time and then released them to reveal them to her.

They were beautiful! He had restored them! The woman was very pretty and the man was full of life. The cares of their past lives had been lifted and grace and love were set in place.

She looked at the treasure hunter again with fresh eyes and suddenly realized who he was. "Jesus!" she exclaimed.

He had promised to journey with her, and had followed the burdens of her heart, searching to relieve them. He had made even the smallest gesture she'd attempted, a prayer or small offering, seem like a great work with enormous results.

"Beloved," He said as He reached out and grabbed her hand, "I have one more thing for you..."

4

THE WEDDING FEAST

Let us be glad and rejoice, and let us give honor to
him. For the time has come for the wedding feast
of the Lamb, and his bride has prepared herself.
—Revelation 19:7 NLT

AS THE TREASURE HUNTER held her hand, a
vision unfolded before her eyes...

She saw an elaborately adorned room in an extremely
luxurious eastern-styled palace. Ornate carpets covered
the floors, lovely ornamental tapestries hung on the
walls and large, embroidered satin pillows covered the
carpet around a magnificent golden table, richly laden
with wonderfully bountiful foods of all varieties.

At one end of the table, she saw a man and a
woman dressed to equal the splendor of the palace. The

gentleman, as rich in his spirit as he was in his attire, was sitting on the pillows awaiting a great feast.

At first, Beloved thought the man was very pleased as he sat awaiting the banquet. But then she saw that, although he was delighted in the feast, the occasion and his apparent opulence, something seemed to trouble him.

His attention was not on the banquet or the room. His full concentration was entirely engaged in the very beautiful woman who seemed to be asleep by his side.

Lying on a sea of pillows near her cherished mate, she was breathtaking in her loveliness. Dressed like a queen in richly adorned frocks, she supported a heavy, golden crown atop her splendid auburn hair. Her bridegroom tried desperately to awaken her, but she remained asleep.

The brilliant pair were meant to celebrate their wedding day with a glorious feast, and he anticipated her awakening. He had long dreamt of sharing this day with her and shook her gently to arouse her from her sleep.

He surveyed the table intently, checking to see that every detail was secured to her liking. Each time he did, it heightened his anticipated joy in her enjoyment of the luxurious banquet they were to share.

The man leaned down and gazed at his beautiful bride. He rested his head on a pillow near her face and smiled. Drinking in her beauty, he tried again to awaken her, but she remained asleep, unable to shake off her slumber.

He decided to gather her in his arms and, holding her against his side, he held her up in an attempt to reveal the glorious wedding feast to her, hoping to dispel her repose. He waved his hand out over the table set before them and whispered, "Darling, our table is ready. All of this is for you, dearest. Please awaken, my love."

His cherished bride tried so hard to stir herself awake but, although she would open her eyes for a short time, her sleep remained. She was soon fast asleep reclining again on the pillows as she had before.

Disappointed, but unrelenting, her bridegroom continued to try to revive her to show her the wedding feast in her honor...

Deeply moved by the vision she had seen and with her hand still held in His, Beloved looked up into Jesus' eyes and, muffling an empathetic cry, she asked Him, "She is Your sleeping bride, isn't she?"

Reassuring her with His gentle smile, He answered. "Yes, Beloved, she is My bride." He continued, "We are waiting for you. Take care and finish your journey."

Matching His assuring smile with her own, Beloved turned back to the fields and continued on, but with renewed and even greater purpose.

He had filled her with such fervency and tenacity, it increased her strength ... she felt stronger than she had ever felt before. The longer she journeyed, the more she could sense His life flowing through her. She was beginning to realize who she was and her destiny in Him.

Beloved was determined she would not fail Him.

5

Meeting Time

The harvest is great, but the workers are few. So
pray to the Lord who is in charge of the harvest;
ask him to send more workers into his fields.
—Luke 10:2 NLT

AS BELOVED CONTINUED her journey
through the fields of grace, the landscape gradually
transformed from fields of wheat to rock-hewn hills
and sand, framing a breathtakingly beautiful sea. By
evening, she saw in the distance the shadow of a great
mountain and was captivated by the reflections of the
moonlight on the water, joined together as though they
were created for each other.

Nearing the mountain, she saw the moonlight
reflecting off a tall and slender human figure moving

back and forth at the base of the mountain. She could see, as she came near, that the figure was indeed a very tall woman who seemed to be lit up from within.

The woman was riddled with anxious excitement and paced back and forth with great haste. Even though she was quite old, she was marvelously beautiful, as though her beauty was captured in time. She wore her splendidly gleaming silver hair loosely curled and flowing down her back.

She was attired in an equally beautiful gown made of ornate, thick velvet. Quite heavy and dark, her gown was embroidered with an elegant, golden-embossed pattern, laden with crystals and decorated with amber and jasper.

While eagerly pacing between the sands of the great sea and the base of the mountain, as if excitedly waiting for someone, she finally caught sight of Beloved and ran to meet her.

Even though they had never met, she spoke as if she knew Beloved quite well. "Beloved, where have you been? I've been waiting such a long time for you to get here," she scolded.

She snatched Beloved by the hand and pulled her toward the mountain with great eagerness, but when she felt Beloved's resistance, she paused.

Suddenly, as if realizing her error, she spoke to Beloved with guarded patience, "Oh, I'm sorry, dear. We honestly have very little time. We must hurry. Everyone is waiting for you." Excitedly, she added, "The Shepherd will be coming soon!"

Time, as she was called, was excitedly waiting for a special assemblage of the prophetic host who were gathering there.

Returning her excitement, Beloved suddenly realized who the lady was. "You are Time!" she exclaimed.

With the sudden revelation of who this beautiful, benevolent creature was, everything began to fall into place. The woman had been pacing back and forth on the sands of time before a small, modest opening to a very large cave nestled in the glorious mountain before her.

"Why, yes, dear. Of course I am, but you are very late and we must hurry," she answered Beloved as she hurried her along.

Realizing she had been led to the very mountain where the much desired host were meeting, Beloved was beside herself with relief.

The Inner Room

Time slipped her arm into Beloved's and quickly ushered her into the narrow entrance of the cave. As she squeezed through the crevice, it opened up to a beautiful, almost ballroom-like cavern with large artistic stalactites hanging from the ceiling like splendid icicle chandeliers.

Amazed at the rustic majesty of the cavern, yet still somewhat bewildered, Beloved wondered, *"Why is it we are in such a hurry?"*

Hearing her thoughts, Time stopped in her tracks and cried, "*Why!* How can you ask *why?* Did you not come through the fields of grace and see the workers there? They are almost out of time – they are exhausted, poor dears. And you ask me why we must hurry?"

Beloved still felt unsure of her purpose there. But Time spoke to her as if she should already know all of what was to occur in their future and why she had been compelled to come to the mountain.

Time's rebuke made her feel chastised, yet she knew it was right. For she had seen the dilemma of the workers in the fields of grace – there were just too few workers, and those who were there were worn out from their heavy workload.

Time ushered her along toward the back of the cave and walked some distance through a long, rough corridor. At last they had finally reached a room nestled deep into the recesses of the great mountain.

They approached a door set into the rock of the cave. It seemed out of place, but Time opened it confidently and ushered Beloved inside.

Unlike the previous caves they had walked through, the inner room was warm and filled with a tangible, glowing amber light. It gave Beloved the feeling of coming home to her well-loved Grandmother's little home.

The room held what seemed to be an intimate group of people sitting patiently while their quiet conversations filled the room with anticipation.

As Beloved entered the room with Time, everyone turned to welcome her and smiled as she entered. Without even letting go of the door, Time turned and addressed the gathering, "There now, she is finally here."

Motioning to the room, she countered Beloved's curious look, "Ah, yes, dear. They will fill you in."

Giving Beloved one last hurried prodding, she turned to leave. "I must continue my watch. There are more to come!"

With that, she was gone and the door closed after her.

6

The Host

"The time promised by God has come at last!"
he announced. "The Kingdom of God is near!
Repent of your sins and believe the Good News!"
—Mark 1:15 NLT

THE WELCOMING ROOM was filled with
women and men of all races and nationalities, both
old and young alike, all of whom possessed the same
warm, welcoming quality that filled the room. They had
been expecting Beloved and stared at her with curious
delight.

Beloved stood timidly as she sheepishly glanced
around the room. Even though she felt she recognized some of the people in the room, she knew she
had never met them. Nonetheless, she was taken aback

when she realized they all seemed to know her and had been anticipating her arrival.

The room was very bright, considering it was inside a mountain. It was filled with a warmth that seemed to penetrate her nerves and quiet her spirit. Beloved fell into an easy repose and knelt comfortably on the floor with the others.

The graciously cheery group welcomed her warmly, as though they had always been friends. Very happy to see her, one by one they introduced themselves and shared their testimonies with her. Each individual held a wealth of personal stories to impart and as they finished, they asked for her to share her story in turn.

Beloved had kept her feelings bottled up inside for so long, now she feared exposing her insecurities and opening herself up to others and their unjust criticisms.

Yet, though she'd only just met them, she felt such intense love and understanding from all of them. The warmth and authenticity that emitted from them seemed to birth a release in her spirit.

An older, beautiful woman named Helen reached out and drew Beloved into her and held her close in a powerful display of sympathy. Brushing her hair, she said, "Beloved, we love you. We who know you, accept you as you are."

Beloved had not allowed herself to realize the pain she had been holding in her heart. She had buried it so deep and tried so hard to keep it hidden, and now suddenly it was awakening with tremendous force. Breaking into heaves of pain-relieving sobs, she slumped to the floor.

The acceptance she felt from the host seemed like heaven filling her heart.

The gathering erupted with tender thanksgiving and filled the room with brilliantly coordinated worship as they welcomed her vulnerability with much needed comfort. Their acceptance and love for Beloved filled the room with a protective shield of restorative power, bringing deliverance for her long-held burdened soul.

Remaining, lingering in a state of unparalleled intimacy with the heavenlies – they all experienced the Father's restoring power. There was something about the mountain that gave them strength and drew from each of them the best of their gifts and help as they ministered comfort and relief to one another.

The room continued to fill as more seekers arrived to join them. And as they delighted in each other, Beloved knew she'd finally found them. She was, indeed, with the much sought after, yet hidden, prophetic host.

THE SHEPHERD'S ARRIVAL

A sweet fragrance filled the room as heaven invaded. Beloved felt a great sense of relief blanket her when Jesus suddenly appeared.

He broke into the middle of their meeting and every eye instantly turned to Him as hearts filled with expectation.

As always, He filled the room with instant delight and, locking eyes with each person, He ignited the fire of the intimacy they each had with Him. He proceeded to express to them the importance of their function in the great battle they would all soon have to face and the significance of this hour.

"The hour is great and there are few of you, but you will find the strength you will need in the harmony you share as you are united in Me."

His heart brimmed with emotion for each of them and the room filled with an intensity of purpose as they realized He was preparing them for battle. "The age we are now entering has been anticipated by the Father from the beginning. We are all excited and are anxious to see Him display His power. He is with us as we fight for Him, as He releases to us the victories of the white-horse rider."

"Before I leave you, there is a very important key you have that you will need to grasp before I can let you go."

They all cried out to Him in earnest, "Please, Lord. Give us the key!"

"But, My friends, you already have it," He delighted to tell them.

They seemed very confused and determined to discover it.

The Lord turned to Beloved as He shared with the room, "Beloved has something to share with you, My friends – the key to your victory in this hour."

"I do?" she anxiously returned, quite startled.

"Yes, Beloved, you do! I gave it to you several years ago. Have you forgotten?"

She struggled to remember, then realized He was referring to a vision He'd shared with her years ago. Oblivious to it's importance, she had held it in her heart until she felt it was needed.

Beloved stood as He reached out His hand to her and took her back into the vision of a very dark place...

7

THE RIVER OF SHAME

Darkness as black as night covers all the nations of the earth, but the glory of the Lord rises and appears over you.   —Isaiah 60:2 NLT

BELOVED FOUND HERSELF with Jesus again – He brought her back to the place He'd shown her previously in a vision...

Beloved, now caught up in spirit with the Lord, remained yet within the inner room and shared the intensity of the darkness the Lord had shown to her. Those assembled listened in anticipation, waiting to receive as Beloved told them of the vision.

She began, "I joined the Lord while He was at a gathering of the saints. I was so happy to see Him.

I rushed to His side and wrapped my arm in His. My whole being came alive in His presence and overflowed with joy. His smile refreshed me. I felt loved, but somehow I knew this would be no ordinary encounter – something was troubling Him.

" 'Come with Me,' He urged. 'I have something I want to show you.'

"I was more than pleased to go with Him and felt no fear when He led me to the embankment of a dark, forbidding river. It looked terrible. I shivered when I realized that everything around us, even the air and sky, seemed to match the river with its feeling of forthcoming dread as we stepped into it.

"The sky darkened and the air grew heavy and thick. An ominous foreboding swept over me and I suddenly felt uncertainty. I stopped with my hand still in His. Naturally, I didn't want to enter such a place, but the Lord beckoned me 'Please come.'

"Jesus wrapped His arm tightly through mine and led me further into the river. The water was tangibly dark with a thick blackness. As if you could reach out and touch its inkiness, the all-consuming cold of the river clung to me and seemed to want to penetrate my soul. As we waded into the water up to our necks, I felt emptiness rising from the vapors of the river.

"Occasionally, I wanted to grab hold of a log I saw floating in the water and cling to it for safety, but Jesus wouldn't let me. I realized there was something in me that did not yet fully trust Him. The fearfulness of the river made me question His goodness toward me, since He was leading me into such a dark and frightful place.

"He felt the thoughts of my heart, but did not rebuke me. He was patient with me in spite of my scattered, fearful feelings, and drew me closer to His side.

"As we walked, I saw people in the water who seemed to dwell in the river, as if they belonged to it. They were alive, yet they seemed lifeless. Surrounding each person were sinister creatures of darkness guarding them, holding them captive to the dark river.

"The demonic creatures possessively held tightly to each human they controlled. It seemed as if it would be easy for the people to have gotten away from the creatures, but they didn't realize this and didn't try to break free from their grasp.

"One particular person watched me walk with Jesus and I saw a jealous longing to be with Jesus in his eyes. I knew he wanted to be walking with Jesus through this dark place. He believed it to be impossible, but continued to watch us longingly. I stared back at the man for some time while I continued to walk with Jesus as He led me through the water.

"We finally reached an embankment and pulled ourselves out of the river, but the black water clung to me as if it were a living creature obeying its master by doing so. Soon, however, the water retreated back into the river and I knew in my heart the Lord had commanded it to do so.

"Once the water had retreated, the Lord raised me to my feet and led me by the hand down the sandy bank of the river. On one side of us was the treacherous black water and on the other, a thick menacing forest. The trees in the forest seemed lifeless with no leaves on them, yet they were alive with a hostile presence of their own.

"The river was repugnant, but not as frightening as the forest, which seemed filled with hatred. Jesus was unmoved by the trees, but their coldness terrified me and He kept me near the river's edge. It was a more difficult and narrow path to follow, but at this time He was keenly focused on the river.

"With my hand in His, I followed Jesus around the edge of the forest until we came to a sharp bend in the river. We came across a small boat tied to a log at the turn in the river. He motioned for me to get in as He untied the boat from its mooring.

"As we entered the boat, I was suddenly able to see the river clearly, and I saw that the water was filled with people. Though they literally surrounded the small boat, they did not seem to understand its purpose. They looked to us for help as we approached them, yet shied away from us when we got near them.

"The river was teeming with people herded like cattle, it seemed to me, smashed together, pushed through the river and crashing into one another without any realization of what they were doing. They were, indeed ... lost. So very lost.

"I looked into the eyes of a young girl close to me near the bank of the river. Her head and one shoulder were poking out of the water, but the rest of her body was covered in the thick demonic shadows of the water. Her eyes were sunken, encrusted with dark, swollen circles around them. Her hair was pitch-black, snarled and matted to her head. Her face was ashen gray and her body was covered in terrible scars.

"She seemed to look at me without seeing me at first and my heart was captivated by an overwhelming, even desperate, compassion for her to awaken to the realization of her situation. I wanted so much for her to know we were there. Suddenly, I saw a flicker of life come into her eyes – a breath of hope.

"As she continued to watch me, I saw a very small light waver in her heart. In response, she tried to raise herself from the water's grip. I saw, as she did, that her hands were held together in front of her, tied with an anguishing knot.

"The creatures around her awakened to the solicitous thought of losing their prey and gripped her hands even tighter, pulling her back down. They began flooding her with shame as she looked again at her hands bound and covered in bloody scars. I watched in anguish as the fog of hopelessness covered her mind, shadowing her from the anticipation of deliverance.

"My heart broke when she moved away from me to hide herself in the converging throng of hopeless victims. I lost her there, but not in my heart – where she was alive and full of life. I saw her past full of years of victimization from a demonized father, an abusive brother, rejection from the church where she'd desired to find love and, finally, convinced of her own unworthiness, attempts of suicide.

"Wanting only to die and not live with the contempt she carried within herself, she tried again and again to end her pain. She didn't care now if she were loved – didn't think she was worthy of being loved. There was no need for others to torment her now; she was well able to torture herself. With drugs, alcohol, and a life of perversion, she abused herself. She let herself be taken by any man as punishment for her past 'sins.'

"It was not her sin that bound her to the river, but shame imposed upon her by others. Still, she was convinced by the multiple creatures entrenched around her, using her, that she was to blame for all that had happened to her. Any attempts to rescue her were successfully perverted by these demonic creatures who were used to push her down even deeper into the river of shame until, at last, she was as much a part of that wretched river as the water itself.

"My eyes then found another woman well advanced in age – her appearance was much the same as the young girl's. She looked at me with a flicker of longing, but then the word *abortion* flashed through her heart and mind, as though it were branded on her forehead. Shame filled her memory with thoughts of her past as I saw flashes of images of unspeakable horror and then years of torment – torment that seemed to follow her like a welcomed friend.

"I saw that many times the Lord had tried to remove this word from her heart, but she refused. Guilt forced her to cling to self-hatred, tying her to her sin as if it defined her existence.

"I then realized the river was teeming with women just like this woman who were held in bondage by their shame because of their guilt, with the word *abortion* consuming and destroying their lives and destinies. Then, suddenly, she pulled away from me and retreated into the throng of people.

"I saw another man watching me from farther up the river and was startled by his intense gaze. He looked desperate. I realized then that there was desperation spreading through the people that seemed to multiply before my eyes.

"I could see the man was completely immobile by what surrounded him. He could not move, but I watched him as he floated by me, pushed by the mob in the river. He was saying something to me, but I could not hear it. I saw only his lips mouthing the words 'Help me!'

"Instantly, my heart jumped to attention and my mind raced to think of what I could do to rescue the man. What did he need saving from? Indeed, though he led so many to the forgiveness he craved, I saw he could not forgive himself. I saw the years that he had spent in the pastorate fleeing from the discovery of his hidden life. Indeed, his double life – the life he did not want to live and the life he longed to truly live.

"He was taken captive by a large demonic creature of lust and perversion that had complete control of him. It sat on his shoulders like a proud, disgusting mass. The creature was prideful of his prize, this poor defeated pastor, whose wife defined sweetness and adored him so much. She prayed with all her heart for God to touch him and make him again into the man she once knew.

" 'Help me!' I saw him say again. My heart was gripped with compassion for him and I cried to the Lord. 'Oh, Jesus,' I cried. 'Can't we help that poor man? Jesus, help him, please.'

"Before Jesus could answer me, the river suddenly came alive with activity. Over my cries to the Lord for help, the creatures in the water began to scream in unintelligible shrieks and howling. The sounds rippled through the water like waves and seemed to be calling something.

"Suddenly, from the sky across the river I saw a massive flying creature. It was enormous and flew with great speed directly at the river. The creatures in the river grew louder and louder with their noise and seemed to be chanting something as they saw it approaching. They were greedy with excitement. The sound of them made me sick.

"The creature flew across the river with a large rock in its tentacles, and suddenly I realized what was about to happen. Anguishing fear gripped me, but there was no time to react.

"I was filled with anger at the creatures in the river who were hungry for destruction. I watched as the disgusting, winged creature flew directly at the pastor and launched his weapon at the man. The man did not even see it – his head was turned toward me as he continued to cry his mournful plea for help.

"I screamed a guttural cry from deep inside me as I saw the creature release the stone and watched as it struck the man directly in the head. In a flash he was gone... under the water... I did not see him emerge again."

8

THE RIVER'S END

Though you were once despised and hated,
with no one traveling through you, I will make
you beautiful forever, a joy to all generations.
—Isaiah 60:15 NLT

BELOVED CONTINUED, "I sat for a moment, unable to breath, paralyzed by the scene I had witnessed. The river seemed to ripple with unholy howls and dark, gleeful jeers. The trees of the forest only a few feet away from us seemed to laugh at me. The wicked flight of the flying creature made them bolder in their contempt. The strong gusts of wind caused by the flying creature blustered through the trees, giving them the appearance of power.

"I grew fearful as I watched them but, without saying a word, Jesus held out His hand and the trees instantly stopped. Looking to Him for guidance, He *seemed* to be unmoved by the shocking scene we'd just witnessed. I was puzzled by His reaction, or lack thereof.

"The more forlorn and despairing the river grew, the more intently Jesus looked out over the horizon at the rising sun. I wondered what it was He saw there.

"As I looked to see what had captured His gaze, I saw what He saw. Far off, away in the distance, I saw the rays of the sun peaking out over the horizon. Though it was still only a dim glow, it seemed almost smothered by a dark mist somehow emanating from the river, as if it were trying to dim the brightness of the sun's rising.

"It was still very dark where we were and the light, at this point, only succeeded in reflecting faintly over the thick membrane of death that covered the river.

"The Lord continued His intense watch of the horizon as the water looked nearly crammed with seemingly lifeless, hopeless people held captive by a horde of demonic creatures.

"With the light of the sun, I felt the most fearful I had yet; with the sun's rays, I could see what was really in the water. An almost overwhelming hopelessness filled my heart now as I saw clearly the condition of the people in the river.

"I saw face after face of hopeless longing as they watched us pass by them in the water. Occasionally, a demonic creature, seeing me, would grab onto the boat and try to climb in. But then, seeing the Lord with me, the creature slithered back down into the water.

"Transfixed by the skyline ahead of us, Jesus was not afraid and did not even seem to notice the water or the activity around us.

"The water in the river at this point was barely visible due to the massive throng of people wedged in it. They were packed together, carried along by the force of the crowd and the demonic creatures that held them captive. The water was moving faster now and the people were pressed together mercilessly, all the time watching me with longing in their eyes.

"At this point, the fog was lifting off the river and the people appeared to have a greater awareness of their surroundings. As we passed by, it looked like a greater number of the river's inhabitants were beginning to sense danger ahead for themselves. It was as if the numbness they had felt gave birth to a sense of foreboding for the coming reality soon to follow.

"More and more, a sense of fear took hold of them. Their dark captors increased in their arrogance over what they had accomplished through the grasp of the river's shame.

"As fear mounted, the river's masses became even more frantic and watched us intently with agonized yearning. I watched them, too, wanting so much to help them but not knowing how. Our boat was moving faster than the current, however, and we soon passed by them.

"My heart was overwhelmed with the gravity of their plight, people being goaded along by demonic creatures bent on their destruction. I tried to scream at them and tell them that they should fight back and get away, but the shame hanging over them perverted my screams into accusations of anger. They looked terrified of me and tried to move away, but they were powerless.

"We traveled some distance on the river when the small boat we rode in stopped and raised itself at the Lord's command to stand near the river's edge and rest in the air over the river's path.

"I watched the river of people as they continued to travel under the water's control. At length, the river was overwhelmed by the magnitude of people in it, all wanting deliverance but not believing it was possible.

"My heart was heavy – I could see an empty hunger in each heart and could feel the horror overtaking them. As I looked across the sea of faces one by one, I was burdened by the emptiness in their eyes. Their life-stories all held similar burdens, with hopelessness running through them. Shame held them captive.

"In actuality, the dark creatures possessed no great power to hold the people captive. But the masses were bound by the shame they had experienced, and they felt helpless to fight it.

"I knew that if they could know Jesus as I did, they would be filled with His joyous love like I was. If they could understand the mysterious love of God, their lives would be full of His purpose for them and the shame would be vanquished. Every terror they'd endured would be used for the glory of the kingdom of heaven.

"As I tried to show them Jesus, in their despair they were frightened of Him. They thought He would hurt them; they could not look at Him without shame and remorse generating terrible pain.

"The chilling winds blowing through that wretched forest made it nearly impossible to help them because of the fear that hung in those damp, black branches. I could see the fear overtake them and freeze cold the sparks of love that flickered in their hearts.

"I cried out again to the Lord and asked, 'Oh, Jesus, what can we do to help these people?'

"I was almost angry with Him now, because I didn't understand why He'd brought me to this place if I could not help the people. I knew there must be a purpose and that He must want me to help them somehow, but how? 'Why wasn't He stopping and helping them,' I wondered in my heart.

"The intensity of His countenance almost frightened me as He continued to stare toward the horizon. I felt that He was directing my attention to follow His gaze. I began to look ahead to see what He was seeing.

"I watched and as I did, my focus was urgently captivated by what I thought I saw up ahead. I stood paralyzed, unable to believe what my eyes were seeing.

"'Noooo!' I cried.

"My heart, once alive with willingness to help, was now drowning in a sense of overwhelming helpless panic – I saw the river's end.

"The end of the river was much more shocking than the river itself. People, masses of people, were being hoarded together and shoved relentlessly over a massive cliff to a bloody, rocky ravine below. Death was the goal.

"It wasn't enough that the enemy was stealing their lives from them, he wanted to assure their eternal death – he wanted their souls.

"Causing them to sin, then enslaving them to shame, he was able to imprison them in a cycle of fear and condemnation in which they were continually abused and ridiculed by those who held them captive and used them like playthings.

"Again and again they were unrelentingly violated until they were numb to the conditions they were living in and the dark forces that could do as they pleased with them, doing all, not just to steal their joy but their very souls. Eternal death was a game to them and they enjoyed playing it.

"I looked back at the river as those nearing the edge watched those at the edge plummet thousands of feet to their deaths. Panic gripped them when they realized there was no way they could escape the same fate. They were doomed to death without deliverance – terror striking yet another blow, without hope.

"Leaving the boat, I ran away from Jesus and back to the river's edge to those I could reach. I began to scream at them – 'Wake up! Stop! Get out!' Anything I could think of to get their attention, but they turned from me frightened even more by my aggressive, panicked countenance.

"I panicked as I tried to think of what could be done for them. I looked to Jesus and He watched me with a look filled with thankful emotion.

"I saw a small crowd of people on the other side of the river. I thought maybe they could help me reach these people, so I hollered to them to get their attention. However, when they looked toward the river, they were filled with disgust at the sight of it. They seemed unconcerned by the condition of the people held captive and were angry with me and even cursed at me.

"Pious revulsion stood before helpless depravity and I watched in disbelief.

"Suddenly, I stepped back and my heart was filled with understanding. This was it! This was the reason Jesus brought me here, why He made me feel the river's darkness and the forest's deception. I knew then the only way I could help the people was to awaken His bride. Without that, there was very little I could do.

"The deep sleep had blinded the bride of Christ, catching them on a wheel of unending routine governed by the concerns of their own heart leading them nowhere.

"It was then that I heard an echo in the wind and felt the warmth of the Lion's fire flow through me as I heard Him speak. 'Awaken, My beautiful ones!' He whispered in joy-filled relief.

"Again and again He spoke a word resounding through my being, 'Awakening,' again and again, just 'Awakening,' as if the universe joined Him in this historical exhortation."

Joined by the prophetic host with her in the inner room of the mountain, Beloved spoke of the Lion's cry to awaken His bride. As their voices echoed the emotional, heartfelt cry of the Lion, together they called out in earnest harmony again and again, "Awakening! Awakening! Awakening..."

The passion for the Lamb's bride that had been imparted to them all had empowered them to bring deliverance to the sleeping bride. As the glorious host wept with the remembrance of the burden they were still facing, they were emboldened by the added newness of the urgency of their call.

9

THE SEASON OF THE KINGDOM

He lets me rest in green meadows; he leads me
beside peaceful streams.   —Psalm 23:2 NLT

THE INCOMPREHENSIBLE COMPASSION
of the Lord, the Father's relentless love for humanity, literally filled the inner room of the mountain as
Beloved and her friends were now submerged in the
transforming power of the Lord's heart.

He spoke to them and flooded their hearts,
"Dear ones," the Lord began, *"I have held you in reserve for
this hour. You will experience the greatest outpouring of My
presence on the earth to this day. It will be ignited by My love*

flowing through you. Guard this love with your whole being, for it is the greatest force on earth. It is the reality of heaven made manifest to the world through you, My dear friends.

"I commission you now to administrate My outpouring on the earth. It is for all men to experience. Although some will not respond well to My presence, they must have the opportunity to know who I Am and what they mean to Me.

"It is both your calling and your great responsibility that they would have the knowledge of who I Am revealed to them. Without the fulfillment of this call, we cannot be together as I wish.

"For some, it will be a time of great pain, but not for you, friends, for you have captivated My heart and will compel many to turn to Me. I have kept the best wine for last, and this wine will complete My will – empowering you to carry out My commission and establishing My kingdom on the earth.

"For as I spoke through Joel, I will truly pour out My spirit on all flesh. I will come, I will release My kingdom and I will have My way – there is no truth to the lies that cause My children to become complacent and forget My commands. I am Lord and I will be Lord on the earth as I am in the heavens. You will share in the joys and victories of this historic season – we will fight together to restore the Father's house and complete His great joy.

"When all is finished, I will reveal Myself to all mankind. They will know I Am who I have declared Myself to be and then the end will come.

"It is then we will enjoy the great wedding feast I have prepared for us. It will truly be a feast of great celebration and fulfillment."

As the Savior gathered His friends and prayed, His body was transfixed and made radiant, emitting glory of unearthly power and force. The room was filled with a burning energy – the power of transmutation. The intense light seemed to explode from inside of Him like an atomic blast, hitting every person in the room with great force.

Empowering them for their mission, His light instantly engulfed them and they appeared as though they were limp human forms held in the grasp of the light's intense power.

Burning and creating, the light transformed them. Working first in their hearts and then through their minds, the light of the Savior created brand new untainted memories out of the painful past events in their lives – transforming them into trophies of grace to be used to impact the children of the earth.

Then, gripping their necks and shooting down through the spine, it continued. The light enveloped each vertebra, penetrating the stomach cavity and shooting out from the arms and legs until it burst forth from their fingertips, even as a star reflects light from the inside out.

As the light rescinded, they returned to their conscious state. He gave each of them an impeccably pure white stone the size of their hand and told them all of the heavenly power it possessed. "This stone has the ability to release the faith of the Kingdom. Strong enough to crush doubt, it has the power to awaken faith, and My faith is the power of the kingdom released for such a time as this – the season of the kingdom."

"One more thing before I release you," Jesus said.

"I have given My life to receive My bride; she is the most treasured possession I have. I, alone will present her to the Father to complete His joy. Yet My great treasure and heaven's anticipated delight has been treated with disdain by many. Brutally and heedlessly, liars have attacked My true followers and they have suffered cruelly.

"Without fear of reprisal, thinking they were for Me, they have slashed at My beautiful bride. Warn those who will repent of My displeasure for their cruel actions, for I will soon shower the unrepentant with terror – they loved to curse, so they will

walk in their curses, chaining them to darkness. I have come to show mercy, I seek even those who would condemn My bride, but My love is accomplished through repentance.

"My dear friends," He continued, "you must tell My bride that it was not I who abused her – I have come to restore her, to fill her with My glory – the glory she was destined to live in. She is My glory and I will restore her!

"Seekers, you must love My bride like I would love her. I am asking you to lay your lives down to see her restored to Me."

10

The Wolves Are Coming

Look, I am sending you out as sheep among wolves. So be as shrewd as snakes and harmless as doves.   —Matthew 10:16 NLT

AS THE PROPHETIC HOST left their comfortable subterranean meeting place, motivated by Time to hurry to those still asleep, they shared such a bond with each other that they did not want to be parted. They formed a kinship which only comes from truly understanding one another through the sharing of similar callings and burdens.

With one final embrace to last them for a long while, they left each other and began the long harrowing journey to the place of their calling. Their minds were filled with all they had shared together with the King, and it took great urging to send them on their way.

As Beloved started on her journey, her thoughts were filled with the life-changing joys she'd experienced in the mountain. The remembrances of the tranquility and harmony of the prophetic host she'd just left continued to flood her thoughts with the warmth of true friendship. Her heart wanted so much to stay, for she had found it to be a place of great safety and comfort.

She reflected on all they had shared together – of the power they'd experienced and, most of all, the treasured friendships that conveyed such powerful acceptance. Truly, it had been a supernatural acceptance which she had previously imagined could only be experienced in heaven.

Traveling past the sandy coast at the base of the mountain, she eyed again, in the distance, the sunny fields of grace she loved so dearly. But the longer she let her mind dwell on her memories of the mountain's treasures, the more the loneliness of the fields of grace became an increasingly stark contrast to the joyous experiences she'd had with her friends.

Beloved longed for the companionship she'd left, and her reflection drifted toward the plight of her friends. It suddenly dawned on her she could travel at least some of the distance *with* her friends. "Yes," she thought, "Why did we part ways so soon? I could travel with them and I would not have to be alone."

Her mind was decided. She would leave the fields of grace and try to find her friends. Heading back up over the forest-covered hills tapering down the mountain, she ventured in her quest. "That's not too far from the fields," she reasoned to herself, "I could surely find my friends there."

With this thought in mind, Beloved determined to give way to the impulse to leave the path that had become so familiar to her, where the Lord had revealed Himself to her in such marvelous ways.

Veering to the left of the fields, Beloved began her climb up a steep, rocky ridge and over a grass-covered bank. The twists and turns the hills took made her question her decision more than once as she regarded the nice level fields below.

After an exhausting climb, she reached the woods she had seen from below, but there was no one in sight. She was quite positive it was in this direction her friends had headed, but it had taken her too long to climb the rocky hillside.

She considered once more returning to the fields of grace, but reasoned her friends could not be far ahead and was determined to find them.

Her journey was growing more and more unfamiliar to her now, which made her unsure of the next direction to venture. Drawn in by the enchanting forest, she was captivated by the woods brimming over with the lush and awe-inspiring greenery she so enjoyed. Oh, how she loved their beauty, and the element of the unknown beguiled Beloved and captivated her yearning for adventure, drawing her deeper into the woods.

The passion she felt that propelled her toward the sleeping saints had dwindled and she was now becoming dismally sidetracked from her initial quest by her pursuit of her friends. Still, pressing on, she was unknowingly led more and more by the dreadful fear of being alone.

Alone though she was, she relished in the breathtaking scenery that brought her such enjoyment. All about her, the flowers filled the woods with a fresh, earthy fragrance.

Caught up in her thoughts, she contemplated how much longer she should continue her pursuit. Then, seemingly out of nowhere, a large man and his wife came running to her. With large eyes and teethy grins they talked smoothly and gave her little time to react or think. They seemed nice, but Beloved felt uneasy. Yet the couple quickly overwhelmed her fears with the easy friendship she so desired.

They told her they'd been wandering alone in the woods in a quest to find blessedness. The couple seemed to have sacrificed a great deal as they sought the enlightenment they said they desired. A tale of continuous, painful struggles and rejection flowed from them, as a well rehearsed river eventually wears down rock. They said they were longing to find the simple love and acceptance Beloved had found and believed God had miraculously sent her to them to show them His love.

"Beloved," the man touted, "We've been waiting our whole lives to meet someone like you." On and on, he gushed his flattery. With an overflowing deluge, he continued with his bombardment of flowery compliments. He and his wife repeatedly chimed their postulations, "*You* are what we need!" and "Only *you* can help us, Beloved!" They continued until they had worn down her uneasy resistance.

Before long, Beloved was easily consumed by their need; she felt such pity for them that she quickly lost sight of the reason and importance of her journey. As they talked with her, her mind grew foggy and she felt unsure of what her true purpose was.

Pressed by the seemingly desperate need of her new "friends," she did not have time to think or reflect. Beloved continually gave of herself to the couple through prayer and endless hours of listening to their lifetime of unfortunate experiences.

However, unbeknownst to her, a good deal of time was passing in her efforts to assist her new companions. Their needs seemed to far exceed her capabilities and she began to feel inadequate in her attempts to help them.

The shifty couple had tapped into the weaknesses of her heart and placated her anxiety. Without thinking as to why, she felt a reactionary impulse to please them, but again and again she failed their expectations of her as each disappointment bruised her spirit. She didn't want to let them down, yet she knew she was.

Her imperfections seemed to mount up before her. The tables abruptly turned on her and she realized that those who had originally needed *her* help and guidance were now instructing her.

They started with insignificant trifles, but quickly moved on to begin their overhaul of her entire personality and calling. The more "error" they found in her, the more she became their captive. Finally, they launched their greatest attack against her: false destiny.

All the Lord found precious in her became an inescapable irritant to the couple.

"Beloved," they screamed, "there is *something* really wrong with you! There is no way you will ever be used by God for anything unless you first fix yourself."

Repeatedly, they berated her, treating her as badly as they could manage. With continuous blow after blow, she had no time to consider the Lord. She felt lost and overwhelmed. Emotionally encumbered by the hopeless lies of their betrayal, she started to reason that death was her only escape.

With her soul clogged by the heavy burdens of their condemnation, she felt numb and her thoughts were lured into a state of chilled emotion. Close to giving up, a powerful voice literally broke into her disparaging thoughts. Her well-loved Guide was speaking boldly into her spirit, "Beloved, look closely at your new friends. Can you see what they really are?"

As if seeing them for the first time, her eyes were suddenly opened. Beloved pulled back from them and saw in horror ... she had befriended *wolves*.

How could she not have noticed before that their clothing was only a cover-up for their true identity?

They were not friends at all – they were deceivers sent to entangle her in anything other than her true destiny.

Their cruelty had blinded her, yet she could see plainly now how little they resembled humans. Truly, they were employed by another realm – the realm of darkness and deception that had so overtaken those caught in the deep sleep.

All at once the remembrance of the sleeping saints hit her heart like pangs of piercing guilt and fear. While she had been running from her destiny, caught in the deception of the wolves, others had been waiting for her – truly needing her desperately.

A well of panicked emotions erupted inside her and she immediately looked for a way of escape from the grasp of her deceivers, but she feared it would not be easy. She knew they would be relentless in their possession of her God-given destiny.

They would, she thought, continue to successfully delude her. Her panic threw her into a state of anxious despair. Vehemently, she hunted for a place to hide. In her emotionally weakened condition, she felt she could not stand against them on her own – she longed for the Rock of the Lord she'd left in the fields of grace and frantically looked around her for help.

"Hide me, Jesus!" she screamed.

"Is there anywhere to hide in this place?" Her apprehension tormented her. "Lord, where are You?!"

Yet there was no place to hide here. Beloved had left the fields of grace to follow her own way. Now, she needed grace so desperately.

"Would He meet me in this place?"

Suddenly, stilled by an intensely supernatural peace, at last Beloved realized there was no other way to leave except to confront her abusers.

Sighing, she dropped her shoulders. Confrontation was the thing she feared more than anything...

THE SWORD OF THE LORD

For with fire and with his sword the LORD will
execute judgment on all people.

                                        —Isaiah 66:16 NIV

BELOVED'S DESIRE to pursue her friends from
the mountain she loved had diminished. She no longer
feared the loneliness she had dreaded. Now, solitude
seemed to her something to be relished.

Indeed, all the previous concerns of her heart were
overshadowed by the extraordinary yearning she felt for
her dearest Lord. She gave way to drifting memories,
clung to the remembrance of her cherished times with

Jesus, and felt her strength being renewed in the memories of His love for her.

Resolute passion began to fill her again. She would seek Him anew, bolstered by a supernatural strength that was not her own. He had filled her with His strength, empowering her to face the deception that loomed over her.

She would, indeed, confront the wolves.

She returned her attention to the oppressive presence of her captors, and immediately the wolves sensed there had been a change in their once spiritless prisoner. They stared at her again with their misleading smiles as they assumed a contrived, presumptive guise.

Strengthened by the Lord, Beloved stood her ground. "You have tried to drive me away from my Lord!" she resisted them.

Trying to make her point, she attempted to continue, but was cut off. Erupting like a volcano of relentless, calculated lies, they chose indignant outrage to combat her defiance.

"How dare you speak to us like that," they hissed like snakes.

Still trying to cover their true identities, they continued their deception. "We are your covering! We truly care about you and you are being ungrateful for *all* we have done for you."

Had Beloved previously been suffering from any remaining self doubt, her eyes were completely open now. Truly, the wolves themselves were beguiled by their own lies, and she knew nothing she would say to them would move them. Indeed, nothing else mattered to them except maintaining their own deception – they were incapable of empathy.

Beloved stood her ground. Regardless of whether they believed her or not, she would speak the truth for the sake of her own soul. "You are liars and I will not listen to you anymore!" she retorted.

Seeing that Beloved was much stronger than they had previously anticipated, they altered their tactics and fought against her with fear and intimidation. Trying to regain control, they screamed at her. "If you leave us, you will go to hell!" they warned.

"We are going to tell everyone what a rebellious person you are. We will tell it all – we are going to warn the world about you!" They continued to intimidate her.

Fear began to seep into Beloved's tender heart and confusion attempted to overtake her mind again. She sank to the ground and cried. Trying hard to shut out their accusations against her, she only succeeded in numbing her mind.

Bombarded by regret, she cried out. "Oh, God! Forgive me, Lord. Rescue me and help me, my Dearest," she wept. "I am Yours and always have been. Oh, God, help me!" she continued to pray as she broke into unrestrained sobs.

Her enemies only laughed at her and mocked her sincerity, but she did not hear them. Her heart began to give way to despair, and the deep sleep loomed over her like a deceptive dream trying to take possession of her once again.

"No more," she lamented. "I want no more of this. I will not help anyone – I cannot help them! I can go no further. I'm done..." Thoughts pelted her numbing mind.

All at once, she felt a powerful hand on her shoulder. She checked her tears and whirled around to see who had gripped her.

She gasped, and peace flooded her heart. The radiant angelic had returned to her, though truly they had never left her side. Instantly, she felt their comfort. In her woundedness, the well-loved angelic reassured her she was, indeed, not alone in her fight and they had called in supernatural reinforcements.

O

It was then she saw the heavenly warrior. He was a towering angel, even more radiant and glorious than the angelic who were with her. Manifesting great power, the warrior filled the forest with light. He stood between Beloved and the arrogant wolves. Obvious terror struck the wolves as they attempted to display a defiant resistance yet were crippled by the impact of the terrifying light.

Stupefied by the heavenly appearance, Beloved stood paralyzed and unable to react. Slowly, as she was able to absorb the reality of what was happening, she was overwhelmed with fright for her enemies.

The great warrior drew his flaming sword and, reflecting the fire it burnished, it gave off a piercing light. Casting aside the oppressive shadows of the forest, it illuminated the darkness. Throwing off the night like ancient grave clothes, it banished the storm, bringing deliverance to her captive heart.

Sudden realization struck Beloved like a sea and she wondered at the sight of what was about to occur. "Can it be God's will to destroy them?"

She heard the warrior speak in answer to the question of her heart, "I have been given authority to execute the judgments of the Lord."

Raising his arms, the warrior raised his sword and thrust it into the wolves.

Beloved cringed and braced herself. She couldn't watch.

The warrior knew Beloved's thoughts and spoke to her again, "This sword is the sword of Truth and will dispel the lies of darkness that have taken over their souls."

She looked at the sword and saw that in its radiance, it seemed to be alive and was pulsating. As its large blade rested in them, the Light it held began to fill them; like melting gold, the Light seeped into their chest and penetrated their hearts.

At first, they lay motionless as if the sword had destroyed them, but she then saw them cringe as if in pain. Watching their faces contort, she sensed brokenness entering them. As they were filled with the heavenly fire, grief invaded their souls as truth penetrated their hearts.

Beloved stood watching the heavenly warrior when she was reminded of the angelic still with her. Calling her back to herself with a reassuring embrace, the angelic urged her emphatically, "Run now, Beloved!"

She had been so wrapped up in what was taking place, she had not considered herself. Recalling her dilemma, she knew that now was her moment to escape and find her path once again.

As Beloved ran, she was still plagued by the disparaging lies implanted in her soul from the deceiving couple who'd held her captive.

At times, it so overwhelmed her that it seemed to consume her thoughts as she rushed blindly through the woods. She searched endlessly for the fields of grace, compelled almost completely by the need in her own heart. With each step, she knew she was getting closer to the grace she longed for and the healing she desperately needed.

With a measured distance between her captors and herself, she wrestled with the fear that clawed at her heart. She wanted to trust again and find that easy repose she once had with the angelic who were trying to lead her.

Beloved had escaped the ambush of the wolves, but a propensity to fearfulness clung to her soul.

Angelic Restoration

Then I looked up and saw two women flying toward us, gliding on the wind. They had wings like a stork, and they picked up the basket and flew into the sky.　　　—Zechariah 5:9 NLT

BELOVED REALIZED her battle was now inside her. The wolves had done their work. They had planted seeds of rotten fruit that tried to take control of her soul and destroy her destiny. It was too late to regret her decision to leave the fields of grace. She had to focus on survival if she was to champion her thoughts.

The wolves had caused fear to root deeply in her soul and it was an unnerving force. The slightest hint of danger would send her reeling. The angelic fought continually to guide her, redirecting her focus, but were limited by her greatly diminished faith. Again and again, fear overwhelmed her emotions as she heedlessly ran from the help she desperately needed.

Suddenly, a thick menacing mist invaded the woods, surrounding Beloved with an oppressive heaviness that terrified her. Feeding her terror and overwhelming her emotions, she fled from it, sending her charging heedlessly through the woods to escape its dreaded tyranny.

Not knowing how long she had been running, she suddenly stopped when she was startled by the sensation that something unearthly had brushed by her in the fog. As she listened to the deafening silence of the woods, she was sure she had heard the sound of running feet all around her. Around and around she whirled, full of fright, trying to see into the mist.

The threatening sounds of labored breathing and rapid grunting filled Beloved with panic. The atmosphere around her was charged with intensity and she knew she was in danger, but what was chasing her? Sinister flashes unveiled themselves as she caught sight of the unholy creatures attempting to block her way.

Trapped by the mist and overwhelmed with fear, she now found herself pressed from every side by a band of tormenting demonic creatures. Chasing her with their terror, they charged at her relentlessly with their menacing lies and malicious accusations.

Beloved tried to defend herself, but they appeared to her like the ominous cover of mist, blending in with it and blinding her vision – crushing her peace. They were incessant. Like a dripping faucet they pressed in on her, coming back again and again with destructive lies. Trying to rip at her mind with seductions of dissembling defeat, berating her with overwhelming persuasions of self hatred, they were determined to take possession of her. She was to them a great prize because the Lord cherished her so much.

Overwhelmed, frightened and crying, she tried to run from them. Yet she seemed helpless to get away. Tormented by their unrelenting indoctrination, she screamed against the dark images, "Leave me alone!" Exasperated, she swung around and attempted to break free from their barricade, just when something extraordinary caught her eye.

It was only for a moment she saw it, but Beloved was quite sure of what she had seen. She was surprised by the failure of one dark creature; he had shown his true emotion and she had seen it. Just a small flicker in his beady eyes was enough to capture her attention. It vanished as quickly as it had appeared, but there was no question in her mind. She had seen a glimmer of fear in one of the creatures chasing her and it disarmed the lies of accusations entangling her.

Beloved was amazed by their error, but it was too late. She had seen what they had been desperate to conceal from her. Their power was raised by the fear they inflicted, and she saw now how important her fear was in empowering their lies against her – her fear gave them control. Without fear's premise, they knew she could easily overpower them. It was, indeed, *they* who were afraid of *her*.

Beloved turned to face them and planted herself defiantly in front of them. "Wait!" she challenged, "You're afraid of me, aren't you?"

"Noooo!" they hissed back at her, repelled by her suggestion.

They tried to hold their ground, but it was too late. She had seen the fear in their eyes.

Wrestling with her thoughts, she questioned in her mind, "What are they afraid of?"

She was puzzled, but in gaining insight, fury began to build within her. Even more so, she was beginning to remember who she really was, and their contemptuous treatment fueled her anger.

"They tormented me and tried to convince me they had all the power," she stormed, "but all along they were the ones who were afraid ... of *me*!"

Fear seemed to rise in the creatures as they watched Beloved's demeanor change. The reality of their power-less condition swept over them and they stood helpless to ensnare her. They could no longer hold her in the torment of the mist.

Beloved watched as fear overwhelmed the minds of the sinister creatures, and it pleased her to realize how threatened they were becoming. She knew now nothing could hold her in their grasp. With determined delight she charged right through the midst of the mob as they screamed their pathetic objections. She was leaving their grasp.

Powerless to hold her, the ambush the enemy had set for her was incapacitated as she embraced the revela-tion of the power she possessed. As the demonic crea-tures realized they could no longer hold her, they fol-lowed her in a feeble attempt to once again gain control over her.

She walked steadily away from them in defiant pur-suit of the path she'd left. Angry at Beloved for her victory over them, the creatures were hungry to continue their assault against her, so they pelted her with their miserable lies once again.

The onslaught of unhappy upbraiding continued as they criticized her every movement. Yet she charged ahead with triumphant determination as her spirit awakened to the true purpose of her battle.

As she tirelessly trudged forward through their disparaging barrage, she suddenly sensed the voice of her constant friend and treasured Guide break into her thoughts. And what He spoke into her spirit made her heart want to soar.

Her precious Holy Spirit resonated in her spirit, "Beloved, you can fly!"

"What?" she asked, as she stopped in her tracks. "I can fly?" she questioned Him.

Suddenly the mist all around her began to clear and she felt something rise up deep inside her soul. She agreed, truly, she was destined to fly. So ... she decided to try...

The creatures continued to accuse her but even as their assaults continued, she made her attempt. At first she flew just a few feet above the ground with the demons following still, but even though she'd flown just a little, she realized she was, indeed, flying!

Beloved was filled with joy. She knew now what her Guide had spoken was true. Yet the creatures tried in vain to turn her first attempt into a failure in her eyes. Boldly they mocked her, laughing hysterically with ridiculously overplayed emotion. She chuckled to herself and turned her gaze toward the sky again.

Undoubtedly, she had been able to fly all along; she just hadn't really understood whose she was and the giftings He had placed inside her. "Could that be what the creatures are afraid of?" she wondered.

"Were they all terrified I would learn the truth about myself? Afraid I would discover that I could fly far away from them?" For truly, however powerful her enemies had been, there would be nothing to tie her to them now.

"They all knew that someday I would, indeed, fly and they were petrified I would soar!"

Once again she attempted to fly and this time, with little effort, she easily flew above them. However, she still continued to struggle in her endeavor to fly away out of their reach. As they continued to attack her, they screamed out accusations of fear and doubt, trying in desperation to recapture her attention with loathsome fear and self-hatred.

"You cannot fly, girl!" They fanatically screeched out their accusations. "No! No! No! Truly – YOU CAN'T

FLY, BELOVED!" They continued to mock her with open disdain, "Who do yoouu think you are, *gggirlll?* Yoouu are nothhinng ... there's something wrong with yoouu, ggirrlll."

In hearing their lies, Beloved felt herself beginning to slip down toward their reach. With each lie, she perceived a danger to her faith, and the distance she'd gained was threatened. A tremor of fear leaped at her heart, putting her closer toward their grasp.

"I can't go back!" Beloved screamed, "I won't!"

Then she heard Holy Spirit whisper softly His faith-building words, "But Beloved, you *are* flying." At the sound of His beautiful voice she felt her heart lift again and fear was thrown back – it was true!

"Yes! I am really flying! I'm doing what they told me I could not do!" With the power of His vital words, she couldn't help but fly a bit higher.

Beloved realized as long as she stayed safe, close to the ground, the creatures would not stop accusing her and she would continue to be in danger of heeding their lies. Again, her gentle Guide strengthened her heart, "Fly *higher*, Beloved."

A surge of faith filled her. "I *can* fly higher!"

Beloved flew high above those forlorn creatures as a well-deserved smile spread across her face. Flying higher, out of their reach, she wanted to soar away from them. Breathing deeply, she closed her eyes and threw back her head. She surged upward toward the open sky. "I will soar!" she cried.

High above the threat of her enemies, she left them far behind her. Trusting in the arms of the One who loved her, the One who'd rescued her from the deep sleep, she opened her heart to all He'd destined her to be. In return for His love, she would love Him back. She would love Him with every breath she breathed, with every beat of her heart – He was her Everything!

13

Heaven's Invasion

Look at them as they leap along the mountaintops.
Listen to the noise they make – like the rumbling
of chariots, like the roar of fire sweeping across a
field of stubble, or like a mighty army moving into
battle.   –Joel 2:5 NLT

SOARING in the heavenlies, filled with the love of
her Savior, Beloved was seeing her life, and the lives
of those she loved, from an entirely different perspective. Seeing clearly now the angelic as she looked to her
right and to her left, she was truly surrounded by beautiful, celestial guardians who had never left her side.
They spoke openly to her now, knowing she would hear
them. Together, they flew at great speed into the atmosphere and to wondrous heights they ascended.

While tied to the earth, she had seen only glimpses of revelation of the Father's victorious kingdom. Now, she saw the expanse of the terrestrial planet clearly through the eyes of faith the Father had given her. Truly, Beloved recognized the extraordinary days of the victorious white horse rider were here at last.

Flying with the angelic, she witnessed great battles being fought all over earth's realm. Indeed, it flooded her heart with joy to see the victorious battles for the exultation of the Prince of Peace. She laughed out loud as she thought, "Wars fought *for peace*," – how ironic. She grasped it all now, "No peace without the battle..." the angelic knew she finally understood.

Beloved could sense in her heart there was a heightened intensity filling earth that had been dulled by apathy for centuries. What a revelation the church was receiving. She could sense the passion for the Lamb beginning to rise. "They *will* love You, Jesus!" she shouted to the Lord. Beloved was undone as she beheld the revelation of the Bridegroom!

There was something new and different Beloved felt in her spirit. Heaven was surging with expectancy – the kingdom of heaven was preparing for an invasion and the realms of earth were left unaware of the nearness of their deliverer.

Light burst through the sky as Beloved's spirit was captivated by an intense feeling of heightened awakening. She felt the anticipation of heaven's determined triumph.

Flashes of chariot wheels exploded in her spirit, turning and twisting in hurried preparation. Horses stopping, grunting their impatience, awaiting the heavenly riders mounting in readiness of the warriors' determined march. In bold resolution, she watched the great army make their preparations for an invasion of huge magnitude. Heaven was preparing to invade earth!

THE PRINCE

Indeed, Heaven was moving closer to earth and walls crumbled in consequence of its nearness. Spiritual walls were responding to His impending arrival. Idols were being demolished in the hearts of believers. Veils disintegrated in anticipation of His eminent coming. With one purpose and one destination, the kingdom of heaven was invading, coming to restore the earth (Revelation 21:5).

Beloved knew that what she was about to experience and what the earth would see revealed was the unequivocal authority of a Prince! THE Prince!

She could feel the weightiness of the roar of the Son of Heaven upon the atmosphere and she watched as earthly kingdoms bent and crumbled like playthings. Earth's idols shattered and the radiance of Holy Spirit was pervading – destroying the strongholds in the minds of men.

Astounded by seeing what she'd previously only dreamed about, Beloved saw the future of the earth revealed before her. The impact of the ancient doors closed long ago now suddenly opened and an entire kingdom of priests were emerging to serve their King in truth and integrity. Seemingly out of nowhere, a great army stood and arose to take up their position for war!

In the heavenlies, she heard the Father's voice roaring like the great waves of the ocean in a torrent. With one word He fractured the skies, in heaven and on earth. He spoke a word of great importance. Like thunder, it reverberated without end. "IMPENDING!" He spoke to the ascendancy of the universe surrounding Him.

Mystified by the scenes being played out before her, Beloved saw those the Father had held in reserve for this hour, those He'd drawn to Himself. His children, *His family*, standing with confident abandon, at the day of their impending destiny – beholding the majesty of their glorious Father's mysterious plan unfold, unveiling His mighty power.

Beloved heard the Father declare from His throne, "Such is the call of earth's Savior. His kingdom will rise to claim His bride. He will manifest His power and authority on the earth."

"My dearest," she heard her Father speak to her, "Do not fear the enemies around you. Look to Me - look to My throne, follow My thoughts. Trust Me - I will be your EVERYTHING!"

14

AWAKEN, MY LOVE

Awake, north wind! Rise up, south wind! Blow
on my garden and spread its fragrance all around.
Come into your garden, my love; taste its finest
fruits.   —Song of Solomon 4:16 NLT

IN FIGHTING many battles for her Prince, Beloved
was now a formidable force for anyone who came against
her. Transformed by her deliverance, she embraced the
purpose for her journey and the battles she had faced.
Made fearless by her struggles, she feared nothing, for
she knew the power of her King.

He had become her strength, her delight and her
deliverer. Following Him now without question, she
even enjoyed the battles He allowed her to fight in. She
was learning to expect the victories brought by the white

horse rider – indeed, it was the season of great victories, and the enemy swiftly scattered at her command.

Beloved had been awaiting the Lord's arrival in the garden of His making. He'd told her to meet Him there, that He had something He wanted to share with her. Her expectancy was growing and she wondered, after all she'd been through, what would the Shepherd have to share with her now?

As she played with the question in her heart, she waited breathlessly for Jesus to come. Anticipating the joy the garden possessed, Beloved's heart felt overwhelmed by the Lord's delight to share this special moment with her.

In the midst of the garden the Lord appeared to Beloved and opened up a vision in the spirit realm to show her. She saw a captivating young woman clothed as a bride laying on a bed in the middle of the same garden she was now in. Her hair was long and thick in a mass of curls spread out perfectly around her face and shoulders like a dark amber cloud. Her head was adorned with a simple white garland of lilies, seeming to belong to her like the thick tresses of her hair.

Beloved was captivated by her beauty; it took her breath away. Admiring her, she contemplated, "She is absolutely the most beautiful bride I have ever seen."

The bride lay like a portrait in peaceful tranquility on the cushioned bed surrounded by the artistic garden made to frame her. Her long, thick lashes and full red lips rested stilly, while her flowing, white chiffon gown lay perfectly spread about her as she slept.

Everything about the bride exuded purity – uncluttered beauty unlike anything Beloved had ever seen.

As Beloved watched in anticipation, Jesus entered the vision and approached the bride as she slept. With awaited purpose, He stared at His sleeping bride. Kneeling down next to her, He took her hand as He spoke gently to her, *"Awaken, my love. It is time to awaken."*

As she opened her eyes and sat up in her bed, the Bridegroom stood back to watch her awaken. The bride looked at Jesus with expectation and stood to her feet. She looked searchingly at herself, straightening her dress. Rightly fixing her hair, she seemed to dust off the remnants of her slumber. When she was quite certain she was ready, she looked at the Lord with eyes rich with anticipated love.

She ran to Him and threw her arms around His neck in an unbridled playful way, yet exuding such sweet, tender love for Him - how happy she was that He had awakened her. Still clinging to Him, she hung her head back and gazed into His eyes. Her eyes spoke of a deep well of the most pure and innocent love.

Suddenly, she pulled back from Him with her eyes closed and face raised to His. She was completely filled with love for Him and her affection was evident through the joy that flooded her face. So full of such a wonderful, incredible, indescribable devotion, she let loose of Him and twirled around in front of Him as if to enjoy the love she felt. He laughed gleefully as He watched her adoringly.

She ran to embrace Him again. As they held each other, a bright, piercing light burst forth from inside her. Her body was soon enveloped completely by a glorious heavenly light. It exploded forth from her and filled the garden where they were. With eyes closed, head raised and arms outstretched in front of Jesus, she stood illumined by the powerful light shining from her.

Coming from deep inside her, four silvery-white birds burst outward and flew in all directions. They surged upward in flight, soaring rapidly over the face of the earth, covering mountains, oceans, cities and plains. They carried with them the same radiating light that emanated from the bride. Soon, the powerful, life-filling light was saturating the globe.

The bride and her Bridegroom remained in the garden adoring one another, as she glowed with the light of His love. He was not surprised by her beauty, but completely proud of her. He had always seen her beauty, and now the world would be captivated by her as she radiated His majesty.

He knew, at last, she was truly and completely His, assured that, in her eyes, there was no one else – she saw only Him. Saturated in the confidence of His love for her, His passionate love possessed her and she was illuminated by His glory – a tangible expression of His love.

Beloved, now on her knees weeping, felt His joy made complete in the majesty of His bride, over-whelmed with emotion as she watched in the vision her well-loved Savior finally receive His beloved bride.

Radiant and powerful, she was truly His glory. He had won her and together they would reign as the Father intended they should.

The Father's mysterious plan was made complete in them.

To be continued...

In Closing

Dear Saints,

You are the bride of the Lamb. The world has yet to see your beauty and to feel the waves of piercing glory that will burst forth from your love for your Bridegroom – Jesus.

The Father's heart for humanity is made tangible to the world by the light of His love emanating through you. That love WILL spread to the farthest corners of the earth, canvassing it in His glory.

—Victoria

OTHER BOOKS BY VICTORIA BOYSON:

 THE BIRTH OF YOUR DESTINY

 HIS PASSIONATE PURSUIT

To contact the author or to order more copies of
AWAKENING: THE DEEP SLEEP, please visit her website
at www.victoriaboyson.com.

AWAKENING: THE DEEP SLEEP is also available through
Amazon.com, Christian bookstores, and other online
bookstores.

Follow Victoria Boyson on Facebook and Twitter.

Check out the many resources on her website and sign
up for her enewsletter at www.victoriaboyson.com.